Ghost Hous

Emily Butler

abuddhapress@yahoo.com

Alien Buddha Press 2022

©™®

Emily Butler 2022

ISBN: 9798847234894

Language: is it fun to watch

But it is even more fun to play

— ANNA MOSCHOVAKIS

Used and Unused

You like to hear your own thoughts, which is why you've tried to give up every
screen, but they are necessary for many jobs. Jobs necessary for many items.
Many items necessary.

Please provide an itemized list for reimbursement.
Include: unsolicited gift notebooks both used and unused.
Their half-scratched orange price tags.
Their covers of birds or flowers, etc.
Please calculate your total dawns and dusks. If these numbers match, move on to
question three.

At your most recent dusk, you:

      A.   Reminisced about a previous dusk.
      B.   Wished you were alone.
      C.   Wished you were not alone.
      D.   Noticed a new shade of magenta.

Please notice the new shade of magenta.

Notice chirping birds and the way you've enabled a dislodgement
of thought. It is pleasurable to imagine the conversation with the therapist
before the conversation occurs. You consider what you will say
but you do not consider what she will say. In person, she disrupts the fantasy
even as you try to slide it so carefully into place.

The Sky Alone

In lieu of therapy, attend a meditation group.
Spend some time alone at dusk.
Let the rectangles remain black.

In lieu of therapy, perform a comedic routine.
Put yourself in the pillory.
Don't worry, it's not a euphemism.

_____ called, they want their _____ back.

I like my men/women like I like my coffee:
with some kind of non-dairy, alternative milk.

Comedians are insufferable. And yet they suffer. They suffer.

Nevertheless the black rectangle.
You do not need to touch it.
The sky alone makes stars.

Salt

The "why" still stings my throat like bile
nine years later. If it were only about violence
why not pick a bar fight instead? If it were about power
as so many claim, why bother choosing someone you're attracted to?
No, rape is not sex. But let's not pretend it doesn't feel good
for the rapist. Let's not act as if that's not
the biggest reason–
        because I wanted to
It sounds so simple when you put it that way, so easy.
Candy melting in your mouth before you even realize
a decision has been made to grab it from the jar.
Hiding inside the passive voice.

Maybe they rape to ensure we spend the rest of our lives thinking about them
while they go about theirs as if nothing has happened–
        Flipping over the cereal box
        to check its sugar content.
        Greeting coworkers with a smile
        and news of their weekend.
        Tucking their children (oh, Christ,
        they have children) into bed.
        Kissing their wives (who must not know.
        Surely they must not know) on the head.
never once thinking of us.

We, whose senses are tethered to knife-sharp memory.
They turn our favorite melodies to skeletons. For me,
it is the ghostly shift of summer into fall. Oysters and cocktails
in a dimly lit bar. Manhattans and moonlit rivers– ruined.
Most of all, I miss him. That's the hardest part
to say. He's the one I want to comfort me
for his mistakes. The performance would feel so damn symmetrical,
the perfect coda (gentle embrace), the finality
of the sustain (apology), the closure of applause (recognition).
Standing ovation with no encore. Bow, curtain, dimming light.

There is no moment of my life I've played over more than this one,
as if an explanation might be found in the exactitude of details.
I was wearing blue jeans, brown shirt, a style popular then–
long sleeves stitched onto short ones, creating the illusion of layers.
It had mushrooms on it– the drug kind– because I was young
and edgy. I wore no bra and felt his eyes on me
but they didn't sting. I had no wounds yet for him to thrust into the sea.
We talked about gender and oysters. Men's affinity for salt.
I told him about my breakup, which I'd conducted earlier
that day, from the guy he'd never liked.

He did not comfort me the way I wanted or expected,
so why would he do that now? Later, the porch, the river. Moonlight,
or probably not. Probably that is me trying to lend the scene
some false beauty, stitching my sadness to the night.
More likely, flickering porch light, bugs thwacking against it.
Was it even summer, or is that another revision? "Can I kiss you?"
he asked, far too soon. More than anything, I remember his words:
"I'm not going to sleep here" (the couch, where I'd cried myself
to sleep before he shook me awake) "but you're welcome to sleep
with me" (in his bed, past the door he closed behind us).

His ceiling had these thick rafters he liked to joke about hanging himself from
because he was young and edgy, too (younger than I am now, older than I was then)
and I am not the only sad person in this story.
Then, hands. Wet lips a labyrinth. Could he not see my tears in the dark?
Could he not taste them? Oh, men– their affinity for salt.
"This feels rapey," he said.
"It's okay," I said. "It's okay."
Have I lost your sympathy with this admission?
Or had I lost it already, at mention of cocktails and no bra?

Okay
INFORMAL
   Exclamation
        Used to express assent, agreement, or acceptance
           "Okay, I give in"

   Adjective
        Satisfactory but not exceptional
           "The sex was okay but she just kind of laid there"

        (of a person) in a satisfactory physical or mental state
           "I'm okay I'm okay I'm okay I'm okay I'm okay I'm okay I'm—"

        Permissible, allowable
              … "It's okay"

I did not manage to extract a "no"
from the ocean of my hot nauseous belly
but I managed to whisper, "I don't normally do this
without a condom." A box of them sat open beside us.
He never bothered to reach for it as he reached for me
instead. He stopped– no coda. No sustain.
Have I lost your sympathy?

The next morning, I slept late, woke beside his theatrical grin.
He appraised my naked body in tender two o'clock light before landing
on my face and recognizing, in Internet speak, "You has a sad."

Empathetic the way a mirror is empathetic. I stumbled to his yard
where I hid in the foxtrot fountain grass. Tears feel best
in the summer– shivering contrast of liquid and heat–
drying on skin like saltwater at the beach–
when it feels like the sun is ignoring you,
or saying:

Your sadness is not big enough
to revise the sky. There is a whole world outside
of you, waking to their own precious days.
You haven't stopped the earth from turning.
Very little– in the grand scheme– has even changed.

Yellow Jacket

I have this bowl in the shape of an elephant. No, not that kind of bowl.
Not that kind of elephant.

In college I ate spaghetti and chicken nuggets.
I shared a room with one to three other people at any given time.
I always intended to fix the backyard swing but made no plans
to learn to cook anything besides spaghetti.

I walked three miles into town when the buses stopped running. I was no good
at not picturing an elephant. I had no interest in the present moment.
I had a reputation for clashing flannel
with patterned dresses. I had this distinct yellow jacket.
He liked the jacket. He said, "In it, I can see you coming."

Try not to write about writing. Try not to picture this elephant.
Try not to hear his voice
in any key.

Try not to find the narcissist interesting.
Try not to categorize manipulation as genius.
Try not to picture his smile in hindsight as a black and white documentary.

Yellow House / Red House

I.

His house was this indistinct yellow. I couldn't see it coming
as I walked over the bridge towards it, surrounded as it was
by so much untamed growth.
I could see the river from the porch, however,
swollen with accumulating rain.

His house was this indistinct yellow but the ~~night he raped me~~ last night I spent
there, it was red.
I could not stop thinking about it. He painted the house.
How dare he paint the house.

II.

I have this recurring dream.

I dream a new past into a false present.
I see my old friend / rapist. I have forgotten what he did.

I say: *Good to see you, it's been so long...*
Can we talk?

He says: *Sure, but not right now.*
There is always somewhere else
he needs to be.

I never see these dreams coming.
In them, I am so happy. I wake up
so sad. People hardly ever notice
that they're dreaming.
They just say: *Oh, look, a dancing piano*, or
Sure, we can talk.

Yellow House / Red House

I don't know many women who try to make their addictions poetic. Not everything can be interesting. Develop every bad habit of the artist and you will have... what? A whole lot of illegible notebooks. I try not to find the narcissist interesting. I try not to be the interesting narcissist. I write a book of poetry about him. I spend years reminiscing about his disgusting apartment. A lack of privacy is inherent in that kind of mess. Helping him move, I found restraints and cuffs. I found some pretty impressive drawings, but not very many of them. A downright rug of dirty laundry and spare change. Money he would have thrown in the trash had I not pocketed it. Ever-growing pile of pizza boxes and empty whiskey bottles. What do you think– interesting? How about this: Every day I pulled the blinds up. Every day he pulled them down.

Lost Trees

Squirrels seem to know where they are going.
Have you ever, returning to nature,
thought, how did I get so far from home?
Here, won't you help this ant cross the street? A street is a freak
of nature. Millions of installations remain unlabeled.
Manipulation is a category of genius.
As in the painter. As in the trees.

Sound Meditation

Tune your attention to sounds. All sounds.
    Breeze. Traffic. A craving for the ocean.
      Lawn mower. Woodpecker. Breathing.
Focus on your breathing.
    It takes effort not to focus on the lawn mower.
      The man mowing the lawn may be focusing
on the lawn mower, may be focusing on his breathing.

Try not to label any sounds
    (this is impossible)
      those high-pitched chirps are eighth notes:
one e and a two e and a three.

My brother likes to quiz people on tonal intervals
    using birds. There is this bird in Massachusetts.
      I don't know what it looks like
or its name. It calls out four notes:
    a perfect fifth, a minor third.

Male birds learn to sing from their fathers.
    Researchers once gave testosterone
      to female canaries, causing them to sing.
Many species develop regional dialects.
    Like folk music, birdsong is passed down through generations,
      ever-changing. Now, return your attention
to your breath. Do not criticize your mind
    for wandering. The mind, it wanders.
      The birds, they sing.

Fairy House

It is my job to count the fairies in the house. This is not stated, more, implied.
There is a ladder leading out the window. I follow it and forget my job because
you are handing me a pill bottle filled with sunflower seeds. I look different.
You look the same. The pink flags on these lawns signify something political
but I'm not sure what. I walk and the world creates itself around me. I cannot
walk fast enough to get to the end of this simulation– piercing the boundary of
what I thought to be the sky.

Sinedu's Letter

Sigh after sigh I realize–
the flowers keep on dying.
Birds make no difference.

I'm laughing on thin air.
There is a sensation
like falling.
I know that soon
the earth will break me.

A blushing little thing
shrinking ever smaller.
Invisible in crowds.
Choking on river water.

The house was a sunflower. Now it bleeds.
I wait to hear from you.

Cento for Jenny and Jennifer

It's become just like a chemical stress.
Someone shouts "you're ugly." Dogs bark at the sunset.
All these eighties movies houses drown
in purple light. The sky is a bluish gray.
I cry into my hands.
I cry into a pillow.
In my dreams, I see myself hitting a baseball
in a green field somewhere near a freeway.
I walk next to the freeway and down the hill.
Back at home I think I feel an earthquake
and we'd better hurry up. I avoid the mirror again
and then I look in the mirror for what feels like two minutes
but is closer to an hour, tracing the lines in my face
for something more beautiful than is there.
I remember all the women who have not made it.
I've barely been gone.
I think about not making it.
Am I asleep or awake? Where is the song? The beauty?
The movement? The playfulness? The life?
The crowds keep me coming back, cheering.
I've become just like a terrible mess,
commanding the wrong body
the wrong voice
the wrong name.
I'm not a failure, I swear–
I've got a lot over here without you,
but now I want it all for myself.

Scent Meditation

Find a comfortable, symmetrical position on this lawn chair.
Might I suggest resting the soles of your feet on the bottom rung
of the wooden chair in front of you. Yes, the one you found
on the street and painted baby blue but it's still ugly and
chipped from the rain. Do not chide yourself for forgetting
your possessions in the rain: bike, fire pit, hammock.

Now, close your eyes. Someone else will have to read this to you.
There you go. Inhale deeply. Recall the time when your therapist
read you a body scan meditation. You felt so completely
watched. She told you to exhale through your mouth, so you did.
It was uncomfortable. Exhale however you damn well please.
Inhale through your nostrils. Notice any scents.

Earlier, doing the dishes, you got deja vu
while calculating how many more days
your boyfriend will be travelling.

The neighbor's radio static sounds unnervingly similar
to those experimental bands you like. Broken Social Scene.
Múm. Oh, now you've done it. You're only supposed to reference
myths or the Bible. You aren't supposed to make
the dual "you" so obvious.

You aren't subtle. But the smell of your cut lawn is. Inhale it.
Notice how each inhale smells a little different, almost imperceptibly,
but it's there– like the differences in each and every moment
of your life. Each and every bite of your boyfriend's
chocolate cake. Notice how you've never noticed this before.
Now, sniff your own armpit and remember you're alive.

Progress

Tonight, I attempt to calm myself
around the predictable weight
of a nail polish bottle. Shade
black as pupils. Butyl acetate
stings my nostrils. I can't stop myself
from thinking of chemicals
as unnatural. As if the world
were not made of carbon.
Toxic scents trigger pleasant memories:
Gas pumps, road trips.
Energy drinks, all-nighters.
Bleach, a swimming pool.
Can you believe there was ever a time
we didn't live like this?
I could have mixed beeswax
with orchids, crushed berries against cheeks,
traversed by footfall and horsehoof,
no need for microchip or safety goggle.
Let us forget the word tomorrow.
Sometimes the only way forward
is to turn back.

The Castle

Enter the castle with your mind
reasonably open, but let's not
let grey matter spill out our ears.
When you feel a strong resistance
to advice– that is the good stuff.
Venture down into this
dungeon of connotations.
Listen to the rain water dripping on stone.
The eschaton has started,
though it's just advertisements now.
Reminders to turn your devices off.
The lights have dimmed.
The room's gone quiet.

For birds it is a summer

like any other.
Time to sing
the same songs
in the same trees.
More and more
we envy them
their ignorance.
Their peace.

Clouds marble the sky–
a drop of dye
in a tub of water.
The future isn't what it used to be.
But the sky has always looked
roughly the same.
Stable as my scent
associations. Grass
will always mean
soccer practice.
I pour coconut milk
into a pan
and suddenly
I'm at the beach,
lathering sunscreen
to protect myself
from cancer.

I'm tired of writing
about climate change
but it's like trying
not to picture an elephant
when you say "elephant."
It's like trying not to smell soccer
in cut grass.
It's like trying to pretend
I am a bird.

This summer it has stormed
for weeks and weeks. The earth
is angry. And yet, milk thistle
still whispers neutral truths

whenever I devote time
to an empty field.

Terence McKenna said
maybe what we're experiencing
is a kind of birth–
it only looks like disaster
because it isn't finished yet.

Progress II

Skin tight with winter, harpsichord in my veins,
I've forgotten every joy except the smell of dirt.
Opening the curtains lets in the cold.
Closing them shuts out the light.
A gun is inert, and yet, symbolic
of action. It harkens the future. It rains birds
from the sky. What is allowed?
What is allowable?
I'm too tired for history.
Sometimes it is more enjoyable to imagine
than to learn. I want to ask big questions
of small objects, talk philosophy with my socks.
I want a child to run this country,
someone young enough to understand
how simple the solutions truly are.

Meaningless

I open my mouth to speak
and a blue jay flies out instead.
All eyes turn to look at it.
It's like I'm not even here.
I don't want to hunt or farm
but I'd rather not take so many photographs, either,
rather not have to demonstrate my value every quarter,
gather reports, track my moods, exercise, cycle,
diet, water, sleep, and shits.
It doesn't solve anything.
The doctors find nothing on their tests.
It's hard not to hate my body–
the colonies it houses without permission,
our bacterial codependency.
It's hard not to imagine my intestines
as out to get me, hard not to interpret pain, all pain,
as violence. Writing about pain
lends it significance
which is a kind of lie.
It hurts to create (just ask your mother).
I'm dirty with chalk and blood,
exhausted from whittling the world down
to its most salient components:
sandstone, rosewood, calcium,
canvas. My hands reach out to yours,
sticky with paint. Together we make
a brand-new color, one which
only birds can see.

Christening

On the day of my brother's christening
there was a fire at the horse barn down the street.
In the box of photographs, among images
of my parents smiling in wide-rimmed glasses,
holding the mass of my brother shrouded in white,
there is a photograph of a horse, running
against a backdrop of flames.

I wasn't there. But I can imagine it felt
like a bad omen, or at least ruined the atmosphere
of the party. Long floral dresses
smelling like smoke on the drive home.
Uneaten, personalized sheet cake.
It's-a-boy-blue flowers perfectly intact.

But isn't a baby a kind of calamity?
Isn't life a fire no amount of holy water can extinguish?

Love's Altitude

Let us pray.
Let us bushwhack our way around the bog.
Ears popping from love's altitude.
Eyes squinting through fog.

How old were you the first time
you reminisced? On a school trip
in fourth grade, my friends and I talked
all the way to the museum in our sticky bus seats,
about kindergarten. About the day we met.
Memories morphed into lore as we wove
patchwork recollections, creating something new,
something shared. The past suddenly presenting itself
as past.

Let us pray.
Let us bushwhack our way
Through thorny branches
which slice into us, but no harm.
We are protected in our thick, hard coats.
Lead the way by the light
of your head lamp.

That night five years ago
when we bushwhacked
our way around the bog–
the woods were empty
so we ate the mushrooms.
We filled our backpacks
with beer. You led the way
across frozen water.
Everything shifted and swayed.
The night was active, but in my memory
it's still as stone. Still as winter
pretends to be. A cardinal on a cliffside is ornament.
A blessing, this chokecherry tree.

Object Permanence

These new phones are slim, breakable. Smooth as still water.
I crave plastic on plastic, wrapping stiff cord around my finger
like a curl of hair, flirtatiously, though I felt invisible back then
on my parents' porch steps, as far as the cord would take me.
These days I could use something to clutch, something to slam.

With a typewriter, writing was not nearly so clean
or so quiet. I took comfort in the drawers
of the card catalog, reliable and sturdy as a train.
Not even a button is a button anymore.
I visit them at elevators and crosswalks.
I pull them off my sweaters
just to hear them clink together in a box.
I smash this screen to watch it form a web.

Attachment Theory

You've finally finished your elephant drawing.
I can make out the individual pencil strokes. Their diligence
("it took ten hours") comes across as random, as effortless.
You keep your drawings in their sketchbook,
tucked away, unnamed.

I am fluent in language and custom
but still feel sick here.
Open the window. Yes, I know it's hot. But the crickets.
Let's dig our solutions out of the dirt.

Sore muscles are memory.
They hurt me in a proud way.
You bring blood to this brink,
our veins pumping in unison
with shared intent.

I am replaceable, like a machine attachment.
I cannot, however, snuff out one need
by filling another.

It is possible to feel drained but not empty.

It is possible to feel deja vu more often
through drug use, memories barging
into view. Haven't you noticed?
That you've been here before?

#relationshipgoals

Love is distracting.

Love makes it difficult to get work done.

People sometimes say that relationships are work.

They say not to date anyone you work with.

This rule can be "spoken" (as in the employee handbook) or "unspoken" (as in whispering which stops when you enter the room.)

I made a New Year's Resolution to accomplish less this year.

I'm not sure yet if I will accomplish this.

It is best to set goals which are small and objectively measurable.

There is an internet hashtag, "#relationshipgoals," often accompanied by images which are not objectively measurable.

In relationships, I make plans instead of goals– camping, museums, movies, the beach.

Relationships can feel as if they are progressing or devolving– mostly due to the passage of time.

The passage of time can feel fast or slow, although its true rate is objective.

The passage of time is often used as a means of measuring a relationship.

People sometimes ask if a relationship is serious or casual.

Serious and casual are otherwise rarely juxtaposed as mutually exclusive categories.

Jobs are sometimes called casual positions, but they are not called serious positions.

Many professions strike me as quite serious.

I am serious about both love and work.

I am sometimes praised for being a funny person.

A sense of humor is cited as a desirable quality in relationships, though it is not objectively measurable.

Employers sometimes say they want someone with a sense of humor.

A sense of humor could be measured in the number of jokes one makes, or the number of times one laughs.

A man's sense of humor tends to be measured in the number of jokes he makes.

A woman's sense of humor tends to be measured in the number of times she laughs.

The Cabin

Thoughts dissolve.
Atoms shift as smoke–
silver behind fresh eyes.
Each color codependent.

Books claim individuality
but melt and drip off shelves.
Waxen white blinds knock
under false electric wind.
Laughter against the mountain
sways with the cabin.

Knocking at the bench with my knuckles
to sustain a feeling of concrete life.
If our adventure does not commence
here, in a cabin that smells
like crayons and toast–
I'll be translucent with desire.

Will you talk with me about the imperfections of language?

I need to make still these magnetic fields
which feel like infinite wires in my fingers.

Ghost House

There are two ghosts in the house but no one believes me because whenever I have guests over the ghosts pretend to be alive. They do a very convincing job in their party dresses which are quite contemporary because they've come back in style. I fear my personality has fallen out of style. I fear the ghosts will push me down the stairs and everyone will take their side. The ghosts will take my party dresses, my chart of North American butterflies, my second-hand champagne flutes, my many pianos and piano-shaped things.

If, Then

My mind branches like fungi across the forest floor.
The forest will burn, or flood, or heal; it all depends
on which card I draw from this deck. At least
that's what I tell myself. Really, it all depends
on the choices of a couple billionaires I'll never even meet.
I am suffering.
But I still venture out to hear rain smack the street
before it washes away my house, my car, my future
in a rising panic of brown water.
I still stretch my arms towards the calm fire of our only sky.
I am lucky.
The sun is warm, but does not spark. It does us the courtesy
of not exploding. Nothing is hurtling toward the earth.
The sensation of warmth is not the sensation of burning.
It is only adjacent to, only a memory of pain.

Orchard Hill

Spontaneity was easy, then, too easy to even count as such.
It's not hard to drop everything when your hands are already empty,
when the day stretches as far as the horizon. Red wine under an apple tree
in early afternoon. We drank life straight from the bottle,
never bothered with *sláinte* or a speech, didn't even realize we were celebrating
our youth among the rotting fruit in that heady orchard. We cursed
the fallen apples– tiny, bruised, and bitten– as mere lumps in our blankets,
disrupting the comfort of grass. The blades, like everything,
bent to our limbs. The worst of my worries could be articulated
cleanly, bullet points on a To Do list. I knew exactly what I wanted
or so I thought.

The sound of voices and television,
laughter, friendship, possibility–
called to me from where I sat
hunched over a desk
trying to be brilliant.

Freedom was a cigarette and no one to stop me.
Now freedom is the strength to turn them down, even when smoke unfurls
from the prettiest of mouths, its sharp scent sailing me to adolescence,
with all its longings and heat.

In my memory it is always summer, never-ending nocturnes
of moonlight on water lilies and I am surrounded surrounded surrounded.
Lounging on couches in open garages while families walked by,
hurrying their children past the sight of us.
It's not the parties I miss most– but the moment of invitation
when the party still resided in the future, when I hadn't yet said
the stupid thing or stepped in the actual vomit.

Freedom is a synonym for pasture,
for blank calendar, for no calendar at all.
No ticking but the beetles in the meadow.
The abundance of time or better yet–
no concept of it. Perpetual morning,
perpetual night. The second hand smothered to silence
by the stroke of my thick brush, the one with the softest bristles.
Heaven is a spiral, stobelighting between future and past.
Suddenly the swing set. Suddenly your hands, lifting the veil
off my face. No such thing as young or old. No such thing

as lifelong goal, with lifetimes trapped inside each scattered seed,
each speck of dirt glinting off the sun's teeth.

Impossible Things

Teenagers have a talent for making life feel like
a movie. It's a skill we lose with age, like the ability
to learn a language. [   ] delivered all her words
like lines. When I forgot my lunch money,
she covered me, brushing away my thanks.
"Don't think of it as a favor," she said.
"It's a gift."

[   ] liked to drive too fast and blow lines off her copy
of *On the Road*. She closed the distance between irony
and sincerity until I couldn't tell the difference.
She played the bad boy, softened with second-hand sweaters
and light Buddhism. "Maybe I'm *not* Sal,"
she said. "Maybe I'm Moriarty, searching for my lost father."

Her bedroom walls were maroon and covered
in her sketches. She told me not to be like her (read:
starved) which made me want to be like her (hollow, carved
out of light). She was the first person to tell me about the Kinsey scale
but even if she hadn't, her face would have been enough
for me to arrive at the same conclusion.

I loved her. But I did not know this was possible.
So it went the way of impossible things. [   ]
as sepia-toned secret. [   ] as a crowded, lonely party
in my dreams. [   ] as the starlit sky my ceiling keeps
from reach.

The Unconscious Collective

There is no fame in our commune.
Everyone has the same minimalistic bedroom,
the same dim twinkle lights.
Shivering swirls of pink dust
sing to the edges of the past.
Our fireplace is perfect
for the creation of shadows.
We forge memory through forest.
We watch the seasonal retreat of birds.
Much is alive without realizing.
Recede through your mind into a rocking chair.
Recall snow's sophisticated blankness, sudden in your yard.
We've provided several glasses for the smashing.

Emily Butler is the author of Lucid Dreaming, Waking Life: Unlocking the Power of Your Sleep (Toplight Books) and the poetry chapbook, Self Talk (Plan B Press). Their work has appeared or is forthcoming in Painted Bride Quarterly, Spoon River Poetry Review, Cape Cod Poetry Review, ELJ Editions, Anti-Heroin Chic, Halfway Down the Stairs, Bone Parade, Moonglasses, and elsewhere. You can follow them on Twitter @EmilyFButler1

Notes

In 1995, Harvard student Sinedu Tadesse murdered her roommate Trang Ho, then committed suicide. Weeks prior, she sent a letter to dozens of strangers picked out of the phone book. "Sinedu's Letter" is a poem built in part from phrases in her letter.

"Cento for Jenny and Jennifer" is composed of lines from "This is a Poem about the Power of Positive Thinking" by J. Jennifer Espinoza, and lyrics from the song, "My Slumbering Heart," by Rilo Kiley, with alterations made to punctuation, line breaks, and minor words.

Acknowledgements

Thank you to the following magazines where poems have appeared:

The Wire's Dream	The Cabin
Anti-Heroin Chic	Scent Meditation
Emerge Literary Journal	Sinedu's Letter
Spoon River Poetry Review	Ghost House
Lucent Dreaming	The Unconscious Collective
American Writers Review	If / Then, For Birds it is a Summer
The Comstock Review	Progress
Painted Bride Quarterly	Christening, Object Permanence (forthcoming)
Evening Street Review	Meaningless, #relationshipgoals (forthcoming)

Printed in Great Britain
by Amazon

86462109R00031